I'm HERE, Now WHAT?
A journey to regaining balance and stability after a shift in the foundation

By: Vinessia Fisher Hankins

Copyright © 2020 Vinessia Fisher Hankins

All rights reserved.

ISBN: 9798551736738

Dedication

To my Husband, Derrick, for your unwavering Love, Support, and Commitment.
To my Sons, Will and DJ, my two Heartbeats who are my Greatest Motivation.
To my Parents, Isreal and Katie Fisher, I am Because of You.
To my Sister, Sondria, and Brother, Keith, ALWAYS LOVE, nothing else.
To my circle of Family, Friends, and Mentors who have deposited 'gold nuggets' throughout my entire life…'Thank-You'!

If this book in any way impacts your life in a positive way and you begin to experience some of the fulfillments which I have shared through my brief stories herein, then this book will have served its purpose.

Contents

Dedication vii

Acknowledgements xi

Preface 1

[1] Saying Good-bye 4

[2] Getting My House in Order 7

[3] Making New Connections 10

[4] Handling Rejection 13

[5] The Search is Over 16

[6] Feeling Sad and Overwhelmed 20

[7] Just Enjoy Light for Where I'm At 23

[8] My Life Matters 26

[9] My New Family 29

[10] Embracing Life One Day At A Time 33

[11] Feeling The Winds of Change 36

[12] My New Season, I Chose to Keep Moving 40

Acknowledgements

In finalizing this manuscript, I must recognize the following individuals who provided me with their insights, talents, time, and support as I began the process of publishing my first book. Thank you to:

Tiviley Slack, you saw this book in me years before it was ever written. I felt your energy and excitement during our lunch that day as you were offering to be my proof-reader even then.

Joffe Abrom, your commitment and attention to the details of every story during the critical editing phase of my manuscript was simply amazing. I was honored to hear you remember and quote some of my own writings.

Marlene Andersch, I always know that I will receive honest, yet critical feedback which includes thoughtful recommendations that I genuinely value. You are pushing a writer out of a speaker.

Schmella Barney, your expertise in photography is outstanding. You were able to capture my authentic emotions and expressions.

Donzell Newkirk, your suggestions and assistance in Marketing and Advertising were very much appreciated.

Bobby Staten Jr., you were my very first professional mentor and I learned so much from you about navigating Corporate America. Your career advice, work ethics and values were instrumental in my growth and progress during the many years that followed. Thank you for believing in me!

Preface

December 17, 2015…As I sit here thinking about this and that, I realize that it has been 3 months now that I've been unemployed due to a recent layoff at the company where I used to work. Indeed, on September 16, 2015, I said farewell to some of my dearest colleagues many of whom I may possibly never see again. So many emotions and thoughts occurring simultaneously, that the moment felt both exhilarating and somewhat scary. **What** do I do next? **Where** do I go from here? **Who** should I reach out to? **Why** is this happening to me now? **How** do I navigate through this period of unemployment? **STOP!**

UNEMPLOYMENT! Was this really happening to me? Of course, the word itself has become very commonplace within today's society as hundreds of thousands of people are affected yearly by this reality. It is very common for businesses to 'downsize' or as others might say, 'right-size' based on its financial health or strategic priorities. As a former manager, I too have been required to make that difficult decision as to whom to 'let go' more often than I care to remember. One constant thought kept resonating in my mind which is something that I had communicated to many of my 'mentees' over the years, *'this period in your career (life) is merely a stepping stone to a much bigger role (purpose) in your professional journey (destiny)'*. So, do I really believe this or was it merely a 'feel good' message to encourage others? Of course, I do! I think…?? Well, now it was time for me to 'live it' out.

By design, my natural tendency is one in which I see a problem and **quickly** look for ways to solve it, hence, one of the primary reasons for choosing Engineering as my field of study. The mantra that had been engrained within my core being is 'Think…Plan…Do'. 'Why put off till tomorrow what can be done today?' 'Time waits for no one.' 'It's the early bird that gets the worm.' Although my mind was literally racing with so many things to think about, consider, and do; I could hear this faint, quiet voice deep inside of me saying to 'be still'. Wait! Are my senses playing tricks on me? Did I just hear 'BE STILL'?

Now, for those who have spent a considerable amount of time with me either personally or professionally, 'be still' is a phrase somewhat foreign to me. I really cannot remember a period in my life when I wasn't busy doing something. As a young girl growing up, there were of course, household chores, school, clubs, athletics, teaching at church, community service, etc. Then, once I turned 17, I started working part time jobs, continuing my academic endeavors at Florida A&M University receiving both my Bachelor and Masters' degrees in Engineering, and then finally starting my professional career in Corporate America. Indeed, my career did create some sense of security and financial stability for me, and what others might see as a very 'stable foundation'. So now at the age of 46, I find myself in very unfamiliar territory. **I'm Here, Now What?**

[1]

Saying Good-bye

Well, the 30-day notification period was over and **THE DAY** had finally come for me to turn in my laptop and final paperwork and to say 'good-bye' to some of my dearest colleagues, many of whom I may never see again. I actually felt a mix of emotions that morning as I was taking my 'last' drive into work. Although there was much uncertainty about what was next for me, on this particular morning, I was experiencing a bit of anticipation and excitement about starting something new someplace else. As I took that last stroll through the building, there was this 'quiet stillness' that seemed to penetrate throughout the halls and cubicles. This 'familiar' place where I had been working over the past year had now begun to feel 'unfamiliar.' When I looked around, everything was still the same as it had always been, but the difference now was me. I was beginning to change and to see things through a different set of lenses.

After meeting with a few colleagues to say, 'farewell and let's keep in touch', my former executive, Alex, asked me to stop by his office before leaving. Although moments like this are not easy for those impacted by a layoff, colleagues and friends who are still employed also find it somewhat uncomfortable and difficult to hold a conversation. No one really knows quite what to say. My last visit was with Alex who shared with me the story of his wife going through a similar transition a few years earlier and how what appeared to be an unpleasant situation at the time ended up being a pivotal point in her career which worked out very well for her in the end. He offered to provide whatever assistance I may need and a letter of recommendation for any future job prospects. Although I was appreciative of his kind gesture, my mind actually started reminiscing back to much earlier in my career, shortly after I graduated from college, when I tutored Alex's daughter in geometry and watched how she blossomed and grew into a beautiful and bright young lady.

Walking out those doors for the last time, I was reminded of a very popular song by one of my favorite R&B Groups, Boyz to Men, 'It's So Hard, To Say Goodbye, To Yesterday'. The reality was that I would get another job one day; my career would continue someplace else; I would have new colleagues; etc. However, the relationships that had been forged over so many years and the experiences that were instrumental in my growth and development is what caused me to pause and consider this moment. What is my purpose during this transition or 'season' of my life? What is it that I should be doing now? Which direction should I go? **My prayer was 'Lord, please give me enough light for the step I'm on'.** For me that meant, although I may not know what the end of this will look like, I do know that all of this will work out for my good even though it may not 'feel' that way right now.

One of my favorite scriptures that I've practically leaned on most of my life is from Proverbs 3:5-6: 'Trust in the LORD with all your heart and lean not unto your own understanding; In all your ways acknowledge Him, and He shall direct your paths'. *Every ending is also a new beginning, we just don't fully understand it at the time. (Mitch Albom)*

[2]

Getting My House in Order

Now that I was spending a lot more time at home, I started noticing so many more projects that I wanted to complete around the house. Although everything within me was saying to be wise about what and where to spend my money, I kept hearing this quiet voice saying 'live, this too shall pass'. Typically, my natural tendency is to make sure all the necessities are taken care of before acting on any 'wants', especially mine. Now that in and of itself is not a bad thing, but rather wise and makes very good sense to me. However, what had started to become a norm often times left me sad and at times angry because *I chose* to keep putting off some of my own wants and was not experiencing enough satisfaction or joy from the 'fruits of my labor'.

Realizing that I was now in a very different season in my life, one in which I had never experienced before, I purposely made the decision to try and do new things, to act more on my instincts and truly discover a new way of thinking and living. I heard it stated that true growth requires a change in the way a person thinks, acts, and chooses to live. During this time, I found myself rediscovering ME, and I began focusing more on making a life versus making a living.

So, a couple of things which I purchased for the home that were desires of mine for quite some time (actually several years) that I always moved to the 'bottom of my list' were: finding that 'perfect' painting for my piano room; getting that recliner ('my reading chair') for the corner in the master bedroom; putting up more positive affirmations and wall décor throughout our home; creating that study/homework corner in my son's bedroom; completing more landscape projects, painting and the list goes on. Although I started to see more changes occur around me throughout my external environment, I knew that the most important changes were taking place within me. I found myself waking up very early in the morning just to pray, meditate, and read prior to starting my day.

Even when I wanted to sleep in, I could not. Reading became so therapeutic for me that before I even finished one book, I was excited about picking up the next one. And then, there was this very important attitude that I developed about my physical body which was that my physical well-being was just as important as my spiritual and mental health. So, I began walking and running at least 3 times a week with a personal goal of running my first 5K within the next year.

One interesting hobby that I took up during this time was gardening. I began learning about so many different types of plants and flowers also what sort of soil or climate that each would flourish in. For anyone who has spent enough time with me over my lifetime, they know that I have always stated that I do not have a green thumb, and had absolutely no interest in developing one either. My favorite type of plants and flowers were the ones that only required 'dusting off' from time to time. However, interesting enough during this time, I became more and more passionate about watching the growth and development of these plants. Even when some died (and there were many!), I took great interest in understanding 'why' and what adjustments I needed to make in caring for them. Take for instance, the impatiens, it is such a beautiful plant which comes in many different colors. However, one very important fact that I learned was that it requires watering daily, otherwise, it will lose its luster and eventually shrivel up and die. This is unlike the pansy flower that is extremely resilient and can withstand some of the harshest winters. Now, my yellow lily plant was rather interesting to me. I noticed that too much water eventually stifled its growth, but by simply repositioning which part of the plant faced the sun, it caused the yellow lily plant to thrive.

I often heard others talk about their difficulty in caring for roses, but I made it my mission to understand what would make mine flourish. After experiencing some mistakes and growing pains, I learned that the right soil mixed with a little fertilizer and yearly pruning did the trick! It was during this season of my life that I realized how often the 'laws of nature' are used in Holy scriptures to convey spiritual principles about the realities of life. And over the next several months, I would come to see and experience these divine facts within my own life.

[3]

Making New Connections

At this point, I had made updates to my resume well over 10 times, submitted over 30 job applications, but had only received requests for 3 interviews. It was during this time that I began working with Lee Hecht Harrison's Outplacement Services which was a program offered by my former employer. I knew that I did not have to go at this alone, so I decided to seek assistance, guidance, and support from others. My 'unemployment' status was still very new to me and definitely not a position that I would have chosen for myself, but I still made a choice to remain optimistic about what the future would hold. I once heard someone say, *"Embrace change. True success can be defined by our ability to adapt to changing circumstances". (Connie Sky)*

Over the next 4-6 weeks, I attended weekly group discussions and workshops with others who were experiencing the same dilemma as I in searching for that next job. One very important fact which was quite evident during these group discussions was that we all wanted this challenging and most uncomfortable period in our lives to be over sooner rather than later. From resume building, interviewing tips, finding job opportunities, networking, and making new connections, this group started becoming 'helpers one to another'. I found myself no longer consumed with my own situation, but I started becoming more invested in the lives of others by sharing my professional insights based on years of experience and by connecting some in this group to key decision makers at companies that were of interest to them. It was in fact quite fulfilling and uplifting for me to be able to use my own connections in finding potential job opportunities for others.

Although my efforts in assisting others may have appeared to be a noble gesture, I must admit that there were times when I became anxious and wondered when it would happen for me. It was during those moments that I was reminded of the scripture, '*And let us not grow weary while doing good, for in due season we shall reap if we do not lose heart*'. *(Galatians. 6:9)* So, I simply took each day as it came and purposely did those things which were healthy for every aspect of my being, from early morning prayer, to reading various books on different topics, eating healthier, exercising more, meditating while jogging through the park, developing new professional relationships, connecting more with friends/family and picking up a new hobby (gardening). Whatever 'new' idea popped into my mind during this period, I explored it further to see where it would take me. This in turn led me to develop my 'never ending' bucket list of life experiences.

As I look back over this period in my life, I am so glad that I was intentional in making these new connections because there are some individuals whom I now call 'friend' and who I was meant to stay connected to much longer than that one season.

[4]

Handling Rejection

When the month of December rolled in, I was excited for so many reasons. As always, I was looking forward to spending Christmas with my family because I simply love the joy we all experience during this time of the year. Also, I had decided to remain an additional 3 weeks in Pensacola, FL, my childhood hometown, since my youngest son who attended a year-round school in Raleigh, NC would still be 'tracked out', and classes would not start up again until around the third week in January. I was still unemployed during this time, and did not know when I would have the opportunity again to spend this much time with my family. However, my time spent in Pensacola THIS TIME would prove to be very momentous. To state another way, simply 'ordained', which would impact the relationship dynamics and connections within my entire family forever. More details about this will be shared in Chapter 5.

Another reason for my excitement was that I had a couple of potential job prospects, 3 to be exact, which I felt pretty good about. With great anticipation, I was looking forward to seeing how all of this would play out over the next couple of weeks. Here is a general description of each opportunity and the final outcome:

Position 1: Senior Manager Field Support
- Immediate need; expectations high in terms of availability; 60-70 hours workweeks; high pressure environment; role vacant after previous 2 managers left due to health issues
- Outcome: I declined the offer to proceed further in the hiring process.

Position 2: Senior Manager Mobile Development
- HR recruiter moved me to the next phase of the process; 2-3 reschedules with the hiring manager; responses to my email inquiries never returned
- Outcome: Feedback to me more than 2 months later was that another candidate was selected

Position 3: Director IT Program Management
- Moved forward in the process after initial interview with HR recruiter; 2nd interview held with hiring Executive
- Outcome: Feedback 1 month later that another candidate was selected

So, there it was. My excitement at the beginning of the month, left me in a most peculiar state of mind by the end of the month. Although I typically try to find some sort of 'silver lining' even in the most disappointing situations, I was now struggling a bit. My mind was trying to rationalize the fact that businesses tend to put a 'hiring freeze' in place during the last couple of months of the year (something I learned in Corporate America) which would explain why I had not been successful in receiving a viable offer yet. However, before the year came to an end, I had received an email from a new connection (who would later become a friend) stating that she had received an offer and that the start date at her new job would be December 15th! Oh well…there goes my rationale!

So, what would be my 'silver lining' this time? Well, I cannot honestly say that I realized this very important fact then, but I would later come to understand that rejection is not necessarily a bad thing. Sometimes, it's the only way that we will be able to see the other options available to us.

[5]

The Search is Over

When I was a little girl growing up in my household, my siblings and I often heard my Mom talk about how she never knew her Father, but always had that strong desire to not only know who He was, but she also longed for siblings of her own. My Mom was born in Beatrice, AL, and was raised by her Grandfather and Aunts in a household with lots of cousins. Although there was lots of love in her home, my Mom was the only cousin without a sibling which at times made her feel different and alone. Because my Grandmother chose to leave home when my Mom was very young, and did not raise her, there was never really a strong bond formed between the two of them during the early years of my Mom's life. It was not until after high school, when my Mom married my Dad, that their relationship began to develop. This was primarily due to my Mom making the decision not to allow her own personal hurt, disappointment, pain, and anger towards her Mother to interfere with her children bonding with their Grandmother.

Although their relationship began to flourish over the years, my Grandmother still refused to tell my Mom anything about who her Father was, no matter how often she may have asked. To be honest, my Grandmother would get pretty upset if the topic was ever mentioned. It was not until much later in her life when my Grandmother was in declining health that she FINALLY answered my Mom's question. I had told my Mom a couple of years prior that if she really wanted me to search for her Father or any possible siblings, I needed at least a name and the city/state where they had met each other.

After my Grandmother died in July 2011 at the age of 83, my Mom's desire to find out anything about her Father and/or siblings only became more intense. Even though she had mentioned this several times in the past, THIS TIME it was different. So, without informing my Mom, I had made up in my mind that when I returned home to Raleigh, NC after my grandmother's funeral, I would actively start my own research and investigation into finding my Mom's father.

For an entire month, I viewed online databases, court documents, incarceration files, certified deaths, and property records. I even paid for an additional service for 30 days that provided access to additional personal info which may not have been readily available elsewhere. Finally, after seeing the photo of someone who had been incarcerated from an offenders' database, it provided me with the confirmation I needed that I was extremely close to finding my Mom's relatives. You see, the young man in this photo had a very strong resemblance to my younger brother. It was in that moment that I decided to write a letter to four relatives in Lucedale, MS who were all connected somehow either through marriage or biology. I also included a picture of my Mom and myself to emphasize to the receiver of the letter that this was indeed not a hoax.

So, I sent four letters out to these individuals in September 2011 only to receive the same four letters back one month later with the additional message added from the postal service 'return to sender, vacant, unable to forward'. I was crushed because I had such a strong conviction within me that I had finally found my Mom's relatives. Eventually, I told my Mom about the research I had done and the results that followed. That being said, I was still very determined. I had made up in my mind and told my Mom as well, that **ONE DAY** we have to go to Mississippi to see where this research leads us.

So, you may be wondering why am I sharing this bit of history now? Well, it was during this same period during my unemployment that my Mom had met a genealogist named John who had also started assisting her in tracing her Father's family history. Throughout their research, John also had told my Mom that they needed to go to Mississippi. So once that was communicated to me, we decided to take that trip to Lucedale, MS after New Year's Day in January 2015.

THE DAY came, and oh what a day it was! Our first stop was at the courthouse to look through marriage records, and from there we went to the county clerk who managed the property records and deeds. I had brought with me those same four *unopened* letters from 2011 and asked the clerk about those properties and the occupants who lived there. Finally, the 'missing piece' to what had puzzled me for so long! We were informed that a man who lived there had died about a year prior to my letters arriving and that the properties were left vacant. It was at this moment that we knew where we needed to go next, to the only funeral home in town that usually handled the arrangements for African American deaths. Wow, this chapter alone is a book which should be written!

I heard someone state that 'action is what converts human dreams into significance'. So, I'll conclude this chapter by stating that for the next couple of hours, we followed the 'breadcrumbs' (some say 'divine intervention') which were fed to us. Before we left Lucedale, MS later that afternoon to return home, my Mom had spoken to her only living brother on the phone (of course confirmed later by DNA tests)!!! **THIS DAY**, Monday, January 5, 2015 began a new chapter in my family's story.

[6]

Feeling Sad and Overwhelmed

As I sit here now reflecting on this period, I am reminded of the deep heaviness and sleepless nights I had begun to experience. While my efforts to land that next job had increased significantly during this time, there were still no concrete offers made. And since the severance pay that I had received from my previous employer was just about depleted, finding additional sources of income started weighing heavily on my mind. Not only that, but something even more traumatic and personal happened that caused me to sink even lower. The deaths of my uncle, grandmother, and a former colleague all within one month of each other sucked the energy right out of me. I described myself as 'Ms. Weeping Willow' during that period. It did not take much, and the tears would flow!

Throughout my life, I had come to be known as the 'strong one' in my family and close friendships. I was the person who others could rely on for advice or come to for help at any time. Well now, that person was gone. She was nowhere in sight! I was walking around in this fog and did not know what to do next. At some point, I knew I had to snap out of this state of mind and get off this emotional roller coaster. Just for a moment, I wanted, no I needed to be left alone...*I thought*.

The day after my grandmother's funeral, I was checking my email to see if I had received any responses back from some of the job applications submitted or phone interviews. Nothing! But I did notice that I had received a request to speak at a Women In Business Summit at one of the local universities by the Department Chairperson. To say I was a bit surprised is putting it mildly. Of all the times to be asked to speak at a 'Women In Business Summit', I was asked when I was UNEMPLOYED! Two thoughts immediately came to my mind: 1)

God definitely has a 'sense of humor' and 2) I need to respond back NOW, and politely decline this invitation.

But before I acted based on how I was feeling, I took a moment and paused. I began to reflect, not just back over the past 6 months, but back over the times in my life when I felt overwhelmed and wanted to quit. Times when I felt empty, but somehow a measure of strength and grace were poured into me so that I could continue on. Just as rain is needed for the growth and development of what we so often enjoy in nature, it is also needed for our own personal development.

During this moment of reflection, I recalled a word that had come to my mind while driving to the hair salon several months earlier. That word was 'perseverance'. At the time, I wondered where did that thought come from? So, as soon as I sat down under the hair dryer, I googled it to see how others defined the word, and I read 'persistence in doing something despite difficulty or delay in achieving success; synonyms: persistence, tenacity, determination, resolve, staying power, firmness of purpose'. I said to myself back then, 'this is how I want others to see me'.

I responded back to the Department Chair later that evening simply stating 'Yes, it would be an honor'. I had no idea what I would share with those students when the time came, and when I prayed about it later, I only heard 'share your story'.

[7]

Just Enjoy Light for Where I'm At

Well six months later and still no firm offers 'in hand'. Although my remaining severance money was just about depleted, I had made a choice to live each day with no regrets. This was my birthday month (March), and I was looking forward to what each new day would bring.

It was around this time that I connected with an advisor named Barbara from The John Maxwell Team. She had responded to my inquiry about learning more about their program of becoming a Certified Speaker, Trainer and Coach. The discussions between Barbara and myself would serve as another essential point in my journey. We shared some of our life experiences, beliefs, and passions. We even shared a laugh and a tear at times when discussing what motivates and inspires us.

So, on March 3rd, I gave myself the birthday gift of registering for the John Maxwell International Speaker Conference/Training Program which would take place in Orlando, FL that coming August. I chose to invest in myself and my future, regardless of the cost and it felt great! I knew at that moment that this decision would serve a greater purpose than I could even realize. I heard someone state that the principal antidote to fear is ACTION. And oh boy, was I excited about taking this step! I knew deep within me that I was on the right path and had *just enough light for the place I was at*.

The word 'fear' has been described as 'false evidence appearing real' so I was not going to allow the 'unknown' to rob me of the day's wonderful blessings all around me. I deliberately made it a point to make each day count, instead of counting the number of days which had already gone by.

It seemed as though the month of April came quickly which is typically a very active month in my household. First, both of our sons, Will and DJ were born on the same date, April 8th, even though they are 14 years apart! Now, how ironic is that! And, my husband, Derrick and I celebrate our wedding anniversary later in the month, on April 26th.

That year, we decided to spend the weekend at Myrtle Beach for our anniversary. Having grown up in Pensacola, FL, going to the beach with my family was something I experienced quite often. There were many times that I even went alone just to clear my head and to simply listen to the birds chirp and communicate in their own unique language; To feel that cool breeze bounce off of the ocean surface and gently caress across my face as the warmth from the sun beams down on it; And to look over that never ending body of water where the waves would gently beat against the white sandy beach shore just to repeat that cycle over and over again. There was always this calmness and peace that I felt while sitting there and admiring the wonders of God's creation.

Throughout my marriage, I have often seen how excited and intense Derrick would get when planning to surprise me, and I must say, I have never been disappointed! But, for our anniversary this time, I really do not think he even realized just how impactful this 'gift' would be. He has often heard me say over the years that I really wanted to take a helicopter ride even though he had absolutely no interest nor desire in sharing in that experience with me! Something about heights gets to him ('smirk'). Well, to my amazement, we BOTH were about to experience a helicopter ride over Myrtle Beach! I was SOO excited! I felt like a kid in a candy store! Not only was I about to experience a lifelong dream of mine, but the timing of this new adventure felt so surreal.

While up in the air flying over the Atlantic Ocean, all I could do was to look all around me and smile in amazement. My eyes began to tear up as I began to think more deeply about my new experiences and the path which I had started down that was taking me to unknown places. In that moment, I understood even more the statement 'growth takes place outside of one's comfort zone'. It is indeed true, 'failing to grow into new horizons can blind you to the beauty of life's adventures.' I was on an adventure of a lifetime and it felt wonderful! It still amazes me at times when certain scriptures become even more 'real' during certain moments in my life and takes on new meaning, i.e. 'Delight yourself also in the LORD, And He shall give you the desires of your heart.' (Psalms 37:4) I was 'flying high' both literally and figuratively. I was hearing this beautiful melody in my spirit and dancing freely as I allowed my 'dance partner' (God) to take the lead with every step that I took. I felt at peace!

[8]

My Life Matters

As I began thinking about this chapter, I attempted to organize my thoughts in such a way to convey how doing those things which 'feed my soul' has been such a driving force throughout my life. When I have chosen to use my time and resources in helping someone else, I have been simply amazed by the impact of what I consider to be a small gesture of kindness and support. You see, I believe that we were all created for a purpose so much greater than you or I could possibly conceive in its entirety within our own minds.

As I have been faced with different situations along life's way, I have asked myself, 'this is my opportunity, so now, what is my responsibility'? At all times, I want to be authentic, and try my best to leave a situation better off than when I arrived. I do not recall where I first heard this stated, but it is such a powerful statement, 'people may not always remember what you did, but they will remember how you made them feel'!

I recall attending a Leadership Training class during my early years in Corporate America, and a guest speaker posed the following question to the group of attendees which I'll paraphrase as such...'At your funeral, what do you want people to say about you'? Now obviously, no one in that class really wanted to think about their own death, and such a morbid question to ask too!

Well, throughout the years, that question would come back to my mind from time to time. It caused me to pause and to really ask myself:
- What is really important to me?
- Are my actions consistent with what I value most in life?

- What sort of impact do I want to make during my lifetime and beyond?

One thing I know with certainty and that is, I am no 'Florence Nightingale'! Many times throughout my life I acted selfishly, made some bad choices, and frankly, did some 'dumb' things! However, what inspired me the most was when I was able to witness the 'beauty' which came from 'ashes' all because someone decided to do better. I never really answered that question posed to me so long ago…'At your funeral, what do you want people to say about you'? However, on Mother's Day, May 10th 2020, my son Will gave me something so special without even realizing the magnitude that his words would hold for me and possibly someone else…

Happy Mother's Day

The example you've set out in this world has been the driving force that inspires me, and I've loved watching you make things happen, make a difference, and make the world better.

Because of you, I'm not only equipped to claim my own space in the world ~ I'm also deeply motivated. You showed me what is possible, and you built a sense of purpose into my life's foundation.

No mother could be more admired than you, and no one could deserve more thanks and love.

Psalm 16:6 — 'I have a strong inheritance.'

From your son Will

That question was never meant for me to answer, but for me to live! *'When I die, I cannot take with me what I have, but I can live in others by what I gave.'* (John Maxwell)

[9]

My New Family

Well, here we go, road trip! My Dad (nickname 'Chip'), Mom ('Katie'), sister ('Sondria'), brother (nickname 'Keith') and I left our family home in Pensacola, Florida on Saturday, May 28, 2016 around 9:00 AM headed to Lucedale, Mississippi to meet our 'new family' at the Robinson Family Reunion. The distance was about 88 miles and took approximately 1.5 hours. There was much anticipation, excitement, curiosity, and a host of other emotions of what was about to take place over the next several hours.

Thinking back over the past couple of months, I thought about how much I reviewed and studied those DNA results back from Ancestry.com to make sure I understood and believed the data provided BEFORE I shared the results with my Mom. And there it was, at the age of 66, my Mom's only living brother was confirmed! After so many years, prayers and questions were being answered. During the months leading up to the family reunion, my Mom and Uncle CJ would talk practically every day on the phone trying to 'catch up'. They also had met up earlier with their spouses in Mobile, AL to send in their DNA samples together. There was an instant connection between the two of them which made this entire experience for me so surreal!

When we arrived at Uncle CJ's home, cars and people were everywhere! There was so much joy in the air that it was contagious. I immediately went straight to my Uncle CJ to give him a big hug since I already knew what he looked like based on the pictures that he had been sending to me. Before I went to meet and introduce myself to other relatives, I gave two of the four unopened letters that never arrived from years earlier to my uncle. I kept one letter for myself and gave one to my Mom as memorabilia. He simply held them close to his chest and with water in his eyes said, 'I'm going to read them later tonight when I'm alone'.

It was such a beautiful, sunny day in Lucedale, MS! There was lots of good food, laughter, singing and dancing which followed that afternoon. We all simply enjoyed each other's company as we learned so much more about one another and other relatives who were not able to attend. What was so fascinating is that although this was our first-time meeting in person, no one felt like a stranger. Feelings of thanksgiving and gratefulness was felt all around as our families had finally come together after so much time had already passed. What was so touching to see was a sheet cake that my Uncle CJ had made for the event. On the cake was a picture of he and my Mom that was taken a few months earlier when he had visited her for the first time at her home in Pensacola. Over the picture it read, 'Welcome Home Sis'!

The months that followed the family reunion and the connections which had begun was truly heartwarming. Deep relationships started to develop not only with our Uncle CJ, but with his wife, children, and other cousins too. There were frequent communications and visits which continued, from celebrating birthdays to my parents vacationing for a week with my Uncle CJ and his wife, Aunt Sandra. I even had the pleasure of hosting them a few months later at my home in Raleigh, North Carolina in October during their drive back from Virginia. It was truly amazing how emotionally connected we all had become in what seemed to be a relatively short period of time. Often, I would receive texts from my Uncle CJ which expressed his sentiments and just how he was feeling about his life during that time. Such texts read:

"We just started having fun. It's just the beginning. You made everything possible for me and your Mom to have one of the best days of our lives."

"I am still feeling good about having a lovely family added to my life."

"I had a great time with your Mom and Dad. They made me feel like a kid in a candy store. I have a beautiful sister with a beautiful family. Now all of us are one big family."

"You mean the world to me for pursuing me until you found me. I will never forget that."

Although, my Uncle CJ died on December 27, 2016 after battling colon cancer for quite some time, we are forever grateful for the time we were allotted to share in this life with him. The memories created and the time spent together was truly rich. Our families continue to stay connected, visit and share in each other's lives because we understand the blessings that accompany strong family bonds.

[10]

Embracing Life One Day At A Time

Before I knew it, Summer 2016 had begun. DJ had just completed 2nd grade, and I was thrilled that I was able to volunteer at his school's end of year field day event. He was so happy when he saw his Mom helping his classmates rotate to the various stations during the competition or maybe it was simply the fact that he knew he'd be able to leave school early that day and come back home with me. DJ has always been such a very active and energetic kid. Even when he was developing inside my stomach, there was never a time when I was awake that he was not moving. No matter the day nor the hour, when I was pregnant if someone wanted to feel him move, they could. He has brought so much joy and life into our family, and I try to never take for granted this beautiful gift of 'Motherhood' which I have been so blessed to receive twice.

Also, during this time, we celebrated our eldest son, Will's graduation from Guilford Tech Community College with plans to transfer to North Carolina A&T University during the upcoming fall semester. We were extremely proud of Will for this accomplishment! He was beginning to figure out which direction he wanted to go with his education as he was setting off on a particular course for his life. In spite of some temporary setbacks and poor choices earlier on, he made the decision to not give up on his college dreams, and to keep moving forward. C.S. Lewis stated, 'hardships often prepare ordinary people for an extraordinary destiny', and I simply smile when I think about Will's future and the impact that he will make in the lives of so many people.

Although I was still very active in applying for jobs and going on interviews, I tried hard not to allow that activity to consume me. I wanted to be totally present and enjoy each moment when these significant milestones and achievements were taking place in my family's life. Each morning, I tried to embrace everyday with an expectation of something new and good was going to happen. And if I encountered some sort of setback, I decided not to focus too much on 'that thing' which I could not change because I did not want to lose the motivation and energy to do 'those things' that I could change. I still had quite a few more assignments to complete in preparation for the John Maxwell Leadership Conference in August which I believed would prove to be instrumental in my continued growth and development. As he so eloquently states in his book, 15 Invaluable Laws of Growth, 'Motivation gets you going, but Discipline keeps you growing'.

The motivational speaker, Jim Rohn stated, 'Discipline is the bridge between goals and accomplishments' and Vince Lombardi who is widely considered as one of the greatest coaches in the history of the NFL stated "Mental toughness is many things and rather difficult to explain. Its qualities are sacrifice and self-denial. Also, most importantly, it is combined with a perfectly disciplined will that refuses to give in. It's a state of mind – you could call it a character in action."

These writings and so many more served as a constant reminder and catalyst for me to turn any rejection into triumph by continuing to lean forward, learn and find value as I progressed through this 'detour' in my life. I knew that there was purpose for what seemed to be a temporary 'pause' at the moment. Personal growth was indeed taking place outside of my comfort zone as I was beginning to look and move in directions that I had never considered in the past.

[11]

Feeling The Winds of Change

As the month of August rolled in, I began feeling somewhat nostalgic as I looked back over the past year and considered many significant events, new connections made both personally and professionally, and milestones reached. And as I prepared for the upcoming John C. Maxwell Leadership Conference in Orlando, FL, I could not help but to wonder where all of this was leading me? Although I had been experiencing some level of peace and calmness in my life during that time, there was still this lingering question of where my life was headed and why? Because I am a woman of faith and have relied on prayers and holy scriptures throughout my life as a source of strength, comfort and direction for me, I knew it wasn't by 'chance' that I found myself at this particular juncture, but I was here because this is where God wanted me.

When I arrived in Orlando, I was so excited about everything that was going to take place on this week. My curiosity literally had me going on this great adventure both physically and figuratively in my mind. I wanted to digest and experience as much as I could from the information delivered during those workshops, listening to keynote speakers, and making new connections with folks from all over the world. There were over 3,400 participants in attendance who came for various reasons, but one consistent goal shared by everyone was that this was a time to be intentional about investing in oneself.

There were so many 'golden nuggets' shared throughout the week in various forums which were instrumental in causing a shift to take place in my own mind. To name a few…

- 'Faith in the future gives power in the present…'

- 'Potential means that there is more in the future for me than only what is available right now…'
- 'Start leading your life and stop accepting it…'
- 'You don't change people by telling them they are wrong, but by showing them that there is a better way, You be the example…'

It sometimes amazes me how a few simple, yet powerful words can trigger such a dynamic response inside anyone who feeds on them. By allowing these words to take root into the core of one's soul, it creates a growth mindset followed by actions which spawn greatness not only within oneself, but it also spills over into the lives of others. Consequently, this creates an impact far greater than the eye can see.

Although I met so many amazing people, there was one particular guy that I really connected with and this gentleman's name was Glynn. Glynn and I met on the very first day of the conference as we were assembled at the same round table which sat about 10 people total. It was there where each of us had to complete one of our homework assignments which was to prepare a 5-minute monologue on whatever topic of our choosing. To some extent, we were all somewhat nervous with no idea of what the other person would speak on. When it was my time to speak, I remembered what came to my mind months earlier, 'Be authentic, be yourself and tell Your story', which is what I did. To my surprise, everyone at my table clapped, one of the ladies had tears in her eyes, but then Glynn spoke up and asked me to do it again! Now I am thinking, wait, what, why? After I spoke for a second time, Glynn simply stated…'this is not your first rodeo, you are a very polished speaker'. That simple assignment and unexpected compliment would serve as a pivotal moment for me and spark future speaking invitations and workshops just a few months later which I did not foresee coming in that moment.

By the end of that week, I felt both energized and full all at the same time, if that makes any sense. Energized about the plans and actions that I wanted to put into place once I got back home, yet, full in terms of needing to just meditate on the wealth of information that I had consumed over the course of that week. Before I left the conference, I purchased a few of John Maxwell's books, but my favorite was entitled 'The Greatest Story Ever Told' that I bought for my oldest son Will. This is the only book that I have ever purchased filled with blank pages. You may be wondering, so what is so great about that? Inside the cover, John wrote (free handed too!)

Dear Friend,

The Greatest Story Ever Told can only be written by you. I want you to fill these blank pages with intentional acts of kindness that add value to people. Everyday let your words be a record of how you are making a positive difference in the lives of others. Start now and intentionally make a great story with your life.

Your Friend
John Maxwell

We must own our life story! It is not defined by our past and we can write the ending.

On my flight back home, I began sensing a change in the atmosphere all around me. I thought back on the time when I was a little girl growing up and my Dad was showing me how to fly a kite. You had to stand with your back to the wind; hold the kite up by the bridle point and let the line out slowly. The bridle affects how the kite flies and whether it flies at all. If there is sufficient wind, the kite will go right up. My Dad would then let the kite fly away from him a little, then pull in on the line as the kite pointed up so it could climb higher. As I envisioned this kite flying with no specific course nor direction, it was quite reflective of what I was experiencing in that moment. Although now, it would be my Heavenly Father who was holding the bridle, controlling the wind, and determining my course.

[12]

My New Season, I Chose to Keep Moving

As I begin to write the final chapter of this book and consider when this journey first began, I am momentarily at a loss for words as I reflect back over the past 5 years. A shift took place in my life, i.e. 'unemployment', which triggered a series of events, decisions, emotions, and experiences that had been at times overwhelming, yet surreal. I am reminded of a poem which I learned back in grade school many years ago by Robert Frost…

> *Two roads diverged in a yellow wood,*
> *And sorry I could not travel both*
> *And be one traveler, long I stood*
> *And looked down one as far as I could*
> *To where it bent in the undergrowth;*
>
> *Then took the other, as just as fair,*
> *And having perhaps the better claim,*
> *Because it was grassy and wanted wear;*
> *Though as for that the passing there*
> *Had worn them really about the same,*
>
> *And both that morning equally lay*
> *In leaves no step had trodden black.*
> *Oh, I kept the first for another day!*
> *Yet knowing how way leads on to way,*
> *I doubted if I should ever come back.*
>
> *I shall be telling this with a sigh*
> *Somewhere ages and ages hence:*
> *Two roads diverged in a wood, and I—*

I took the one less traveled by,
And that has made all the difference.

I remember so vividly back in September 2016 when I sent out a quick email to a former colleague of mine, Dave, informing him of my interest in a couple of positions at his place of employment. We had worked together in various roles during our time at IBM in years past and had developed a pleasant working relationship with much respect for each other's work ethics. Little did I know, after I woke up from a short nap that afternoon, that a chain of events would quickly start to unfold. Over the next two weeks, I had multiple interviews scheduled across three different organizations at the same company and by the end of this flurry of activity, there were three different job offers for me to consider. As I walked back to my car in the parking lot after a day of interviews, I recall having this amazing peace and calmness to come over me as if to say, this place is where I would continue my career for however long that might be. I do believe that many things in life we decide, but oftentimes we are chosen.

In the poem, "The Road Not Taken", the central theme is that, in life, we are often presented with choices and it is human nature to contemplate the "what if..." about making a different choice. But who knows what the future holds down the road? I strongly believe that *choices and not circumstances determine a person's success (Matt Nathanson)*. There is a quote which I keep over my desk, 'Bloom where you are planted' and for someone to 'bloom', you must be healthy and vibrant! And this is not limited to a position, job title or career, but to every area of one's life.

As I sit here during a new season of my life, I am so grateful that I chose to keep moving and did not get lost and overwhelmed by the shift that took place within and around me. Change is inevitable and never leaves us quite the same. For our own personal growth, we should embrace that shift and let it propel us forward; be adaptable and have fun along the journey of growth and discovery. Sometimes, I felt as though I was losing something really important just to realize later that I was making room for things even greater. Live your best life!

She is Clothed in Strength & Dignity, and she Laughs Without Fear of The Future. *(Proverbs 31:25)*

www.ingramcontent.com/pod-product-compliance
Lightning Source LLC
Chambersburg PA
CBHW031550210526
45464CB00003B/1245